CREATORS' MEMOIRS

WRITERS POUCH

ISBN 979-888555390-2

Contents

1. Amma's Special Box 1
2. A Madrasi's Predicament 4
3. Daddy's Little Girl 6
4. Histories 8
5. Mother's Day 9
6. My First Kiss 11
7. Negative Assumptions 13
8. The Elephant Ride 15
9. The Man Who Called Everyone Shiva 17
10. The Rat Race 19
11. Woman: A Fairy In Disguise 22
12. Winter's Whisper 24

About Contributors 27

About Editors 29

About Photographers 31

About Illustrator 33

About Community 35

CHAPTER I

Amma's Special Box

For as long as I can remember, Amma had a secret special box on the kitchen platform which was always tantalizingly close but was just out of reach. When I was five years of age, I've always wanted nothing more than to open the box and see its mysterious contents.

Nothing seemed fancier to me. Neither the blue flames erupting from the stove nor the sharp knife glinting under the harsh tube light. Even the colourful display of various cereals and pulses didn't draw my attention as much as this box drew me towards it.

In reality, there wasn't anything unique about the way the box looked. It was just like most others. A little steel utensil, plain and unobtrusive. However, it was inconspicuous to everyone except me and so I wanted to know everything it possessed.

My fascination started when I was four years of age. I still remember returning from the hospital after a vaccination. I was bawling and the horrendous hospital smell was everywhere adding to my woes. I was red and misty with chocolate smeared over my round face after my parent's last-ditch attempt to pacify me failed.

My Dad carried me around to divert my attention. He wiped my tears and played with me but I continued screaming. Nothing changed until I smelt a wondrous aroma which made me silent.

I noticed Amma cooking something which sizzled. So I asked my Dad to take me to the kitchen, suspecting it to be the source for the aroma.

There were various vessels placed around the stove with a tray filled with chopped vegetables. I couldn't find the source for the aroma but my father noticed that I was silent and he let me stay there for a while.

It's not like the aroma was a new experience. I must have smelt it many times while I passed the kitchen. Yet that was the moment I realized its true taste.

Even to this day even after twenty years of spouting words and yapping about anything and everything. I'm still unable to describe the aroma that took my breath away and more importantly stopped a tantrum from reaching danger alert levels.

I kept entering the kitchen after my first experience even after my mother denied me from doing so by paying flimsy and random excuses. All I hoped for was to smell the heavenly aroma again.

As the days passed by, unable to figure it out, I questioned my mother about the contents of each box in the kitchen until one day I arrived at the special box. I knew the rest of the contents didn't make this aroma possible based on the little knowledge I had about them.

I had an inkling that maybe the contents of this special box were the cause for my happiness and to my disadvantage, the box was always jutting out of reach and my mother denied to reveal its contents, noticing my undying curiosity and a worrying concern about me harming myself.

In time, I could always see the top lid of the box from my low vantage point. If I stood on my tiptoes, I could even see the special box in all its glory. I could even touch the box by stretching my hands. My fingertips could feel the cold steel after a little effort. With my mother refusing to tell the contents, I wanted to know more about them to know if it is the source behind my heavenly experience.

After being denied for years, I reached an age when I could get a hold of the box myself. After many failed attempts, I held the most curious thing I have always wanted to explore. When I opened the lid, I could rejoice in the scent for a moment before noticing that it was nothing more than a spice box.

A box with compartments to hold commonly used spices like turmeric, cumin, paprika among others. A commonplace and bland box is present in every household. A box that wasn't particularly special except for my fascination. Though it felt anticlimax exploring the contents, it gave me a gateway back to my childhood.

A meandering walk down memory lane, a shot of nostalgia back to simpler times, a reason to smile when cutting onions, a silent hope for the trampled inner child in me and even after all these years, Amma's special box will always be more than just a spice box for me.

CHAPTER II

A Madrasi's Predicament

It is a motley group of 30 people all from different parts, places, areas and walks of life. Yet the minute I stand up and say "Hi! I'm Manognya Bethapudi"

I knew what was going to happen...

A second look followed by filing me in that part of the brain which was related to Idli, Sambhar and more recently Kolaveri Di... ten seconds into the acquaintance and everyone already expects to know from me that I'm a homely, shy girl with a veshti wearing, ash smearing dark and potbellied man for a father and a Kanjeevaram clad Gold bazaar &horticulture endorsement for a mother; pack in Ranji for a brother and there you go!

Its the perfect recipe for a happy little "Madrasi "family from Madras, but unfortunately, they wake up in your neighbourhood every morning to the tune of M.S.Subbalakshmi (obviously)

After they have managed to roll off my phonetic roller coaster of a name (thank god my parents didn't want to take a mini-pilgrimage whenever they called out to me), we get down to hobbies, likes and dislikes. I mention that I like reading and writing... of course, I didn't need to mention it because everyone knows that any Madrasi is extremely studious... Personal inclinations are damned.

By the way, I have to congratulate myself because I just got a new home in a place that's no longer on the map: Madras... No worry if you are from Machilipatnam or from Mangalore, From Karimnagar or from Kanyakumari because you can only come from Madras or compensate for the growing IT industry, Bangalore or maybe even Hyderabad.

Now that you are a stamped-OK Madrasi, be assured that anytime anyone who knows of your heritage encounters any word in any language that might even remotely be south Indian(including the tribal language of

Andaman)you have to give them the meaning.

One fine day, the topic of discussion was none other than women and their myriad hairstyles. As always, it was decided beforehand that I being a Madrasi, couldn't do with other than having well oiled and plaited hair. Moreover, it would be nothing less than blasphemy if I removed even a part of my jewellery (I ask: which)because, after all, it was as necessary to live as the air I breathe.

This reminds me of another basic necessity, Food. You see, we Madrasis eat only Idli, Sambhar and wada along with hot filter coffee at all times of the day. And as my favourite author, "Mr Chetan Bhagat", has kindly pointed out, the guests are always offered noise polluting snake savouries.

I can go on like this forever with instances of blatant ignorance on the part of fellow Indians who, despite liberalization, globalization, Infosys, recession, Unnikrishnan, Dr Devi Shetty and many more, are definitely not ready to accept that a Madrasi a.k.a South Indian is no different than them with the same red blood flowing through their veins and not some spiced up plasma!

Let's hope that in the years to come, people accept a south Indian just as they are... not above them and never below them.

CHAPTER III

Daddy's Little Girl

Out of all the men in the world, daughters always say "Fathers are the sweetest". When I think of my childhood, the first memory I cherish to date is as to how my dad persuaded me to be strong. He wanted me to be a very strong girl.

So when I was four-year-old, I broke a bone in my thumb and it gave me a lot of trouble. The doctors said that there was some minor distortion internally and it must get operated on to get better. Upon hearing this, I reckon my daddy must have lost all his good senses.

Everyone knows how childish men suddenly become after they become fathers to daughters; my father very well epitomized this. It was hard for him to decide what to do. To let his little daughter know the smell of medicines and the pain of toxins, Nah... One day when I went to him complaining about the pain in the thumb finger, he gently made me sit on his lap before saying "Sweetheart, the more you pay attention to the pain, the stronger it would become. So stop thinking about it and one day it will leave you."

Turns out he was right. Well, he always is.

My mother is also a true incarnation of love; for me, she is the most lovable person ever. When I asked my daddy whom he loved more, me or mummy, he immediately replied "He loved me more." and I can vouch that most fathers are like that.

I grew up admiring every aspect of my daddy. He is an energy ball; no matter what happened, I never saw his confidence levels drop even an inch. Now that two decades have passed by, I realise that the love these fathers have for daughters is far greater than what we think. As he walks, sleeps, or even rests, my father's mind and thoughts always orbit around his two daughters. Of course at the envy of my mother...

Even today, when he wakes up late at night, he visits me and my little sister as we sleep. He runs his warm hands over our foreheads and checks the fans and the blankets before standing at a corner glaring at both his daughters. Two of his most worthy possessions before feeling content that he is able to provide us with the comfort of a sound sleep. For a fifty-year-old father of two daughters, that is what it means to be a man and that is what makes them a hero. A hero he truly is! But these fathers aren't as strong and content as they seem to be. They too have problems, unlike us; they have real-serious concerns. So let's not trouble them on little things.

As we grow, we slowly develop differences from our fathers. We start complaining that he checks on us, that he's hesitant to give us pocket money for our expenses, that he is a disinterested person and that he doesn't really understand us. Each time these thoughts strike you, you should know that you are wrong. They understand us to the core. It's their unflinching love for us that sometimes make their actions put us to huge misconceptions. Do not develop hatred for your fathers just because you think they are objecting to a few of your pleasures. They've walked on the planet for half of their lives, they know how things work better than us.

Now that they are growing old day-by-day, year-by-year they need their daughters the most. When else can we reward our fathers better than now and how better can we say thank you to the sacrifices they've made for us every single day than by taking care of them.

If you live with your father right in the same house, then remove your headphones off your ears, switch the apps off your eyes and go sit next to him. Pat him on his shoulder and talk to him about your day's work. Ask him if he's taking his medicines sincerely and give him glasses of water at regular intervals, just like how he gave to you when you were a child.

Become your father's mother, my friend, for tomorrow when his little girl goes her way away from him, to lead her own family, it'll be the poor old father who would feel the greatest void in every breath of his life, more than anyone else.

CHAPTER IV

Histories

It was that time when the headlines screamed of feticide of the female child in Beed district of Maharashtra and during such turbulent times when girls were brutally murdered in their mother's uterus, we were sitting around in the department and talking about the prejudices, discrimination and ignorance of the rural and illiterate folk. In comes Savitribai, the patient allotted to us for history taking.

She looked just like the rest of them, those ignorant fools we were just cursing for killing unborn girls. She was old, withered, in pain and thus started with her long spiel of complaints. By the time we reached the family history, we were pretty sure what her diagnosis might be and we were just going through the motions. She told us that she had 4 children, three daughters and one son.

I scorned them mentally and slotted her to be one of those people who kept trying for a son instead of choosing to have a small family. But she didn't stop at that, maybe my disgusted expression pushed her on. I really don't know but she went on to explain how happy she was with her daughters, how hardworking they were, how much they studied and how proud she was of her daughters and as if this wasn't enough she told us that she would gladly exchange her wayward son for another daughter.

And that was when I realised my folly. I was so prejudiced that I couldn't take people for what they were and assumed that because she was old, ignorant and illiterate. I presumed that she must have prized her son more than her daughters. How wrong was I! Prejudice prevented me from forming a rapport with my patient but the old lady in all her wisdom helped me realise my mistake. But this is just one incident, there are countless others in my fledgeling career and I'm guessing there will be many more in the years to come because while we attempt to take their history and learn about the ailments they end up teaching us life lessons.

CHAPTER V

Mother's Day

It is strange, how I always fail to remember my first memory of you. So, to me, it seems as if you have been with me from the beginning of time. If I recall my first memory of enjoying the warmth of your lap, it reminds me of the night when I had caught cold and you strolled through our rooms, singing me lullabies that I still remember so clearly that I could sing them to my grandchildren. I remember our Sunday meals when we relished your eggplant curry and three eggs as we couldn't afford meat.

While I ate an egg, you would eat half of it for lunch and dinner. It was always a race of who would finish first. You ensured that I won and then offered me a portion of your food. When I grew up a little, you would not do that anymore and if I tried, you would say, "Asking for food from others' plate is bad manners!" Now, at the age of twenty-three, when I think of your plate with half an egg, it makes me realize how you found happiness in that fragment of an egg every weekend. I wish I had at least once, offered you a bite from mine.

You always refused when I'd ask for money to buy ice-creams during the lunch breaks at school. I hated you for that, as I would chew on the sandwich that you made for me. I still remember you saying, "Taking money to school every day, is a bad habit and don't I buy you ice-creams whenever you want them?"

During my exams, you'd wake up with me early in the morning, and sit by my side, when I would revise my lessons. Every five minutes, you'd say, "Study, beta" and slowly doze off on that chair by my study bed. Now when I look back, I see those tired eyes that I failed to notice then. I really bear on me the blame of those black circles which lie under your eyes. Just your presence on those mornings imbued me with the strength to believe that I could continue to do well in school.

When I entered my first monthly cycle, you were the only medicine to my pain and endless worries about my body. You talked me through it, told me how I was growing up into a beautiful young girl. You bought me my first trainer bra, let me be alone when I would shout at you for being around me during my sporadic mood swings. I would be concerned about my pimples, and you'd make me smile by naming each one of them saying, "This one is Puffy, and that one umm...Red Wonder!"

When I'd sleep, you made sure that I carried to my dreams, an impression of your peck imprisoned on my cheek. You wanted me to be a gynaecologist. But when I told you what I really wanted to be, I could see you worried as it wasn't easy for any mother to accept their child being a writer.

My respect for you lies in the fact that you had given me a chance to voice what I wanted. And more than that, you never worried because I wasn't pursuing your dreams. I knew the only thing that bothered you was that writers don't earn much but you valued my passion more than anything else, and perhaps that is why today, I am trying to pen down this piece about you.

Your mortal form might be far away from my reach but you shall always live with me as I share with you an intangible and intricately woven bond!

Happy Mother's Day!

CHAPTER VI

My First Kiss

I don't know who I am. I don't know where I am but I know I'm with someone. It is very dark here. I know that I'm with her and that she is my protector. No matter the amount of pain I cause, she loves me and her love knows no reason.

Till this day, I don't know who I am, but now I can feel my heartbeat because of her. No one on this earth can measure her love. Her love is precious. Yes, I'm in love with her. She's my first love. Many people say that love is a great feeling which comes and goes to every person. Our love is not the love that everyone experiences. Our love doesn't start with each other staring at each other and then continuing as friendship and so on. Our love is blind and unconditional.

Her love is love before first sight. Her love is filled with happiness, pain, tears and for all these, she has a meaning to love. Hers is the purest of pure love. Although I sleep, kick, move or no matter what I do, her heart is full of happiness. She made a world of heaven for me and that is where I live. Our hearts are beating together and we await to see each other. Months passed. I couldn't wait. I started fighting to see her and she understood my desire but couldn't bear my journey. She was crying in a lot of pain, shouting and wailing. Successfully I came to see her. A lot of lulls descended.

She was lying on the bed in an unconscious state while I was wailing to feel her touch. I was lying beside her. The echoes of my cries and my voice hailed into her ears and made her slowly regain consciousness. Her looks started to search for me and as soon as she saw me, tears started spouting from the corner of her eyes. She held me gently in her arm with a grip that steadies and kissed me on my forehead. Once, twice, thrice... and that was my first kiss and she was my mom.

I can never forget my very existence in a deep kiss of hers. Nothing can be more comforting than a mother's kiss. I cherished every one of them and ours is the strongest connection in nature. The bond between us will change over the years, but the strength never fades.

Mom, your love built me a foundation of trust and affection that will last a lifetime. She is the one who takes everyone's place but no one can take her place. No matter the distance, no matter the trouble or the hardship, all will fail before the strength she has provided me. Thank you for showing me grace and thank you, mom, for showering your incredible love towards me.

CHAPTER VII

Negative Assumptions

Did you ever feel like you have been ignored?
Did you ever wish you were someone else?
Did you ever think you were a nobody?
Did you ever feel like you don't deserve to live?
Did you ever feel self-hatred?

If yes, then I'm one among you! If you are thinking if this is self-venting, no it's not! If you are thinking this is 'motivational', maybe slightly. You could be correct.

Let me begin by telling you a story of an unpopular girl who was always with her best friends. She loved them more than anything else and for eleven years, they all studied together. Unfortunately, she had to move to a different school in her 10th grade.

She missed her friends so much that she wrote letters to them and asked a neighbourhood friend who was from the same school as her friends to deliver them. A day later she got confirmation that her letters were received and she felt so happy imagining how her dear friends would feel after reading her letter.

However, months passed by and she got no response. So she wrote letters again but got no response again. This continued for a while before the neighbouring aunty asked, "Don't you think you are acting foolishly? You always send letters and they never respond. Why do you even write when they don't even care?"

Listening to her, the girl felt bad. The happy faces that she imagined all those days, suddenly started looking blank. She didn't know how they felt anymore. However, she wrote again one last time. She wished that the woman was wrong, and desperately wanted to prove her wrong by showing her at least one response.

But she was left disappointed. Years passed and she graduated and started working in a job. However, the fact that she was ignored and the fear of the possibility that her letters were not even read used to make her heart heavy. Once in a while, she cried too.

Yes! That girl is me and I recently found two of those letters that were unposted in my old belongings. I remembered that those were my last letters and I kept a carbon paper while writing the other letters too.

Just as most would, I felt nostalgic. So I took a picture and posted it in my school girls group. Any guesses what happened?

I was ignored again!

I couldn't help but feel bad as nothing changed and none of them cared even now. I didn't open my WhatsApp for the rest of the day, the next day, one of my friends wrote that she collected all my letters addressed to her and saved them at her home. The other girls too recalled that I wrote to them.

I was relieved that at least a few recalled and at least one person still treasures them. For me, that was the most beautiful moment I had in these dark and depressing pandemic times.

Always remember, there's a second side to every story and don't always assume things negatively. If you are going to assume anyway then try assuming positively. If I could have assumed at least once that my friends have enjoyed reading my letters, I wouldn't have suffered all these years thinking I'm unwanted. I wouldn't have this insecurity that I would be a bad friend and eventually, everyone would leave me. Although it looks like a small issue, it can trigger something big inside you. So always think positively.

CHAPTER VIII

The Elephant Ride

Whenever I see an elephant on the road, I feel like giving it a banana or an orange. And I am reminded of a particular episode with an elephant when I was five years old. The schools were closed and my cousins had come to Allahabad for their vacations from Patna. Our daily routine would be a visit to Sangam with grandpa and eat jalebis on our way back home at Hira Halwai which is a sweet shop in Allahabad. Of course, there would be visits to Wheelers or Universal bookshop, Nagars stationery shop or El Chico for pastries, later in the day.

So one day when we had returned from our Sangam visit, I was sitting with my grandmother, and my cousin sister was engrossed in one of her Enid Blyton books. The doorbell rang and we were asked to go out to the verandah.

Grandpa had seen an elephant wallah on the road and had asked him to give me and my cousin a ride. I clearly remember, the elephant was not very old and was not huge. It had a nice padded cushion on its back and a small brass bell tied around its neck. There was a rope around the cushion to ensure it wouldn't divert from its place and I was very excited for the ride.

My excitement ensured that I was fearless in touching the elephant for the first time. As I was small, my grandfather's assistant accompanied me for the ride which was from one gate to the other. And on getting down, I was given an orange by grandpa to feed the elephant which was all the more fun to me.

After me, it was my cousin's turn. She was sceptical about the elephants' behaviour and was trying to excuse herself from riding it. Probably, grandpa had sensed that she was afraid, so he asked her to feed the elephant and as the elephant reached out to get the orange, my cousin shrieked and ran insidc. It seemed silly to me, as to how one could miss a chance of feeding or riding an elephant. However, She kept peeking from behind the curtains.

In order to make her fear go, my grandfather asked her to come and feed the elephant or else he would send the elephant inside the house. At first, my cousin thought it to be a hoax and refused to come out. Then, the elephant wallah was asked to bring the elephant to the verandah. It was fun for me but for my cousin, it was torture.

Anyhow, after much persuasion and lots of surety, my grandpa brought my cousin and made her feed the elephant. She, having fed the elephant with the orange, hesitated to take the ride. I offered to go with her again and got my second ride. After our second ride, the elephant wallah was given some money and rice, and both of them went away. As I bid goodbye to the elephant, I waited in the verandah not only until the elephant was invisible but also till its bell's tinkle got inaudible.

CHAPTER IX

The Man Who Called Everyone Shiva

It was about 8:45 PM, and I was waiting for a bus in order to go home after twelve hours of college. As accustomed, the bus was not going on time. The whole bus stop was free with just three girls, two boys and an old man who sat on the bench at the bus stop. The boys in the group were shouting and laughing while the girls stood whispering. I stood for about half an hour beside the group and was exhausted carrying the heavy bag which had a big fat organic chemistry book in it. I went back and sat on the bench at the stop beside the old Man as there was only one bench left.

All of a sudden out of nowhere came a man who was wearing a saffron colour dhoti and had three horizontal lines on his forehead representing a Shiva's follower. He was naked top except for a chain which had Rudrakshas. He had a turban of the same saffron colour. He was dancing, not even considering his surroundings. Girls who were near the bus stop started smiling by looking at his dance as it is not quite good. I was watching him intensely to comprehend what he was doing and all I understood was a man was dancing that too foolishly.

This man stopped dancing as soon as he could see girls beside him. He shouted immediately "Mata!!! Aashirvaad dho" connotation "Oh Mother, give me your blessings" the girls who contemplation he was barmy as soon as they saw him dancing inveterate it when he shouted.

A girl from the group opened her purse, pulled out a ten-rupee note and pointed it to the man to take it. He did not bother about the note not even for a minute, but he folded his two hands and said again, "Mata! Aashirvaad dho."

Girls did not appreciate what to do. I sat examining him even more fascinatingly. One of the girls turned towards boys expressing for help from this man, while a boy who was watching the whole thing went towards the man responding to her appeal and said, "Paise lekar chale jawo" the man who stood bowed turned up and looked at the boy and shouted "Shiva!!!!!!"

and within no time the man started dancing again.

All of them started laughing at his dance; I also laughed with them. The man danced for a few minutes and left dancing.

The boy who went forward turned back and said, "Pagalwala" all the girls and boys laughed, and I also laughed and said to the old man "Pagal admi hey"

The old man who also watched along with me all the episode said, "He is quite a great man."

I looked at him while the old man continued, "Does pagal means mad?"

I nodded and said, "Yes."

The old man continued, "You think he is mad, but I say we are all mad."

I asked him, "What makes you say that?"

He took a long breath and said, "I don't know whether he is a true sadhu or a fake one, but he had internal joy as you can see him dancing, and you can also observe that he sees god in every human he sees. Show me another man in the whole world happier than him?"

I started thinking about that perspective, and yes, he was right. We talked for a few minutes more about the sadhu, and he said, "I am from India but was raised in England. What I really like in India is the true essence of happiness through religion. Being Indians, I wonder why you people believe in it. What would it really cost? It is just belief."

CHAPTER X

The Rat Race

Winning or achieving by bringing another down,
An evil grin resulting from someone's frown,
Chopping off a King's head to snatch the crown,
Floating on the water by making one drown,
Gives what satisfaction? Compared to a smile from a clown,
Or making our own chocolate cake in a rich brown,
Or stitching for our mother a handmade gown,
Or laying down one's life for saving a whole town!

Welcome to India. The land of spicy food, sarees, billions of Gods, Bollywood, unique culture and whatnot. We have basically everything here! Well, almost. But what we do have, and something which I am personally very proud of since I'm a part of it, are the IITs, the Indian Institutes of Technology. They are the best Engineering colleges in India without hesitation and definitely one among the best in the world. Many in the country want to be a part of these institutes at some part in their lifetime or the other. But the number of IITs are only 16 with a cumulative take-in of nearly 11,000 per year. Since our population is around 120 crores, it is clear that not everyone gets the IIT brand on them.

This leads to the next obvious question: Who are those few? The answer to this is the JEE, arguably the toughest exam in the world. Children now are made to start preparing for it from as early as the 6th grade, when they probably don't even know the expansion of the acronym IIT! This leads to immense cut-throat competition amongst the children to scramble to become one amongst the top 11,000 of the country. The word 'topper' becomes a nickname of sorts which is desired by all but is destined to be given to only one, with the others left in a fit of anger and revenge on that person. It leads to the destruction of many friendships and relationships. The innocent and fragile mind of a child is made to work against their peers and develop a feeling of selfishness.

The children go to really extreme measures due to their immaturity, such as telling a peer that an assignment which was supposed to be given that day has been postponed and that the undoubting peer doesn't submit his paper and loses marks. Another few may also distract their peers during the whole day and prevent them from studying on the eve of an exam but they themselves may have already prepared for the same. Such criminal ideas are not their own, they are induced upon them by parents, teachers and many other factors.

Later on, when they become adults and start working, competitiveness to get a promotion before one's colleagues, office politics, trying to score brownie points with the boss by foul-mouthing fellow employees and other such things are all the result of the competitive rat race mentality. Human beings are the only animals who can effectively communicate with each other at such a highly sophisticated level. But we, instead of working together to improve the world around us, are working against each other to come up on top.

The extent of this mentality is so pathetic and sadistic that some sections of people believe in deriving pleasure from the failure of the other person, even at the cost of their own failure. Can it seriously get any worse! The term "Survival of the fittest" is slowly being turned into "Survival of the contest!"

I understand that not everyone gets everything they want in life, but that doesn't mean you shouldn't let others have it! Instead of wasting your energy on messing up that person's life, if you put a part of that energy in developing and improving your own life and trying to achieve what you want, you will get it! Where there is a will, there will be a way! You just have to look around properly! Have faith in yourself! You can do it!

I made it into IIT Bombay in spite of millions of obstacles like bad friends, girls, movies, Facebook, gaming, texting, WhatsApp, mood swings and every other possible distraction for a teenager, but I made it in the end! If I can, so can you! Nothing is impossible until you decide it is, and your decisions aren't valid until you've tried! So go for it, don't think about what the others are up to, you decide for yourself what is right and what is not. Achieving something by suppressing someone has no high in it, but struggling hard, losing blood, sweat, food and sleep over it and finally achieving it has that feeling with it which is greater than the achievement itself!

CHAPTER XI

Woman: A Fairy in Disguise

A woman is revered as a Goddess in ancient times. But in recent times is she still a Goddess? Is she seen as an epitome to represent a nation? Is she still considered as a nation's pride? Not anymore. Rather than perceive her as a harbinger of happiness, she is seen as an albatross in the whole world. Her life has become worse than purgatory.

The beleaguered women have no ray of hope or no reason for happiness. This is an occurrence in Bihar where many female babies are killed after birth. There was a woman who always dreamt of a baby girl when she was pregnant. Later she dreamt of the baby saying that she doesn't want to come out into this merciless world. She doesn't want to become a burden to her family and she doesn't want to be killed as soon as she comes into this brutal world. She didn't want her baby to suffer, so she hanged herself the next day.

This is the plight of many women across various parts of the world. Her life is in peril. Every minute, every second she leads a spasmodic and erratic life. Every day we come across how women suspected of infidelity are killed brutally. The world is having a heaving dearth of chivalrous men. But she never raised her voice against the brutality she undergoes. She still waits for a new scintillation to come into her life with a hope for mirth and gaiety to enter her life.

But it's high time where women have to raise their voice against these callous deeds. How long will she wait for someone to bulwark her all the time? Although these days, we see women working equally along with men in urban areas, the women in the countryside are still forbidden to decide about their life. Awareness needs to be created among these country people so that they would encourage their own creed. I remember reading an article in a magazine that said "There was an 18-year-old girl who always dreamt of her successful future but no one encouraged her. Seeing her zeal in studies and the desire to accomplish her dream, the head of the village asked her what she wanted to pursue. She said she wants to become a doctor and treat all the people of her village with the best she could. To her delight, he told her that he would make her realize her dream, but she lamented that no one in the village was with her to achieve her goal. He fought against all those people. Finally, after a long brawl, they agreed. He, along with the helping hand of all villagers, were ready to help her. Her joy knew no bounds. She worked hard to become a doctor. One fine day, she returned to her village as a doctor. She was the first girl in the village to study medicine. She thanked that village head from the core of her heart. Now she is a successful woman."

We generally see and read many such stories about a few women who reached the pinnacle despite the unavoidable circumstances. As they say "Where there is a will there's a way". But it's quite excruciating to know that women are not instigated to study even in educated families and are married off at a young age. Remember that all the humans in the world are given the freedom to realize their dreams, then why not women.

Without a woman, there is no successful man, if not a crucial part she might have at least instigated him to do something. Never make her feel that she is an encumbrance to this world. It's not required to worship her. At least treat her as a human. We need to acknowledge the unknown sacrifices which she has rendered to us.

CHAPTER XII

Winter's Whisper

Exactly two months before I was getting ready to leave for Germany to start my masters, my elder brother told me, "Everything changes once you leave home. It is like breaking out of the cocoon hoping to enjoy the colourful world. But only when you fly will you understand that home was a lot better. Mark my words brother. Beauty isn't about the colour or elements around you but the self-discipline and inner peace within you."

As I listened very keenly, he continued, "I might not have travelled around the world but I have been in a hostel for many years now. Always remember no matter how bad things get around you, never give up and always try learning the best from everything."

In the process of getting ready, I bought jeans for the first time in my life. Twenty-one years in India and I never needed the thick bottoms that would take away so much of my pleasure. Hugging my parents as they embraced me back, I left with my sister who was pursuing her PhD in Germany.

Everything was new, right from the cold climate to the new language. Never in my life did I wear so many clothes to just stop shivering in the cold winds. In India, we presume summers are the worst; maybe because most of us haven't felt anything close to winters in Germany.

The first two days I did nothing but stay indoors enjoying the warmth from the heaters but on the third day, something curious happened. On our evening walk to Leipzig's city centre, I could observe the divided roads beside the footpath like our highways. There was a path for the bicycles, beside the bicycles path was the path for the cars and beside the cars was the path for the trams. The wide roads helped every vehicle share its own space.

Though the city didn't have a lot of magnificent stone buildings, the few which existed were phenomenal. Walking in the cold winds wearing a thick black coat, I travelled along with my sister and brother-in-law. Before long, we reached one of the best buildings in the city which was the Deutsche Bank. I couldn't help but feel that it resembled Gringotts. I've even mentioned to my sister, "Perhaps Rowling took inspiration."

As we continued walking, I felt a little more sun wouldn't hurt. Maybe because the grey clouds weren't helpful at all and I couldn't imagine being alone in Freiburg in such a depressing climate. Though my sister tried to tell me about the black forest in Freiburg and the city's ideal location in reaching both France and Switzerland, I've got my reservations.

So a few steps later, we reached "Peek and Cloppenburg" the store where we planned to buy a winter collection of shoes and jackets before it got even colder in December which was just three months away. However before we walked in, I heard a woman singing as she sat before the store. Her voice was as sweet as honey and she played the piano as well.

Honestly, what she sang made no sense to me but somehow I could admire the beauty of it. I loved listening to her so much that I stood in the small crowd before her for a long time and noticed that people were dropping coppers in the hat before her.

I waited for a while to see if she would end so that I could place some money but neither did she stop nor did she take a moment to peek at the coppers she had earned. All she did was enjoy the cold wind and sing songs that meant many different things to her audience. I felt she was lost in her own paradise and I was pleased as to how much she enjoyed her work. She was in a blissful state.

For me, it felt as if her voice and the piano were whispering the truth of life. That night I could still listen to her before I fell asleep.

Until we started our journey to Freiburg, I did visit the city centre as many times as I could just to listen to her. It felt like winter whispering the mysterious beauty of a noble soul.

About Contributors

1. **Jayshree Majji**
   Contributor of "Daddy's Little Girl"

   Jayshree has been a member of the community since 2014 and she writes experiences. Her works can be accessed at writerspouch.com/profile/48

2. **Manognya Bethapudi**
   Contributor of "Amma's Special Box", "A Madrasi's Predicament" & "Histories"

   Manognya has been a member of the community since 2014 and she writes short stories & flash fiction. Her works can be accessed at writerspouch.com/profile/9

3. **Mounika Kodeboina**
   Contributor of "My First Kiss"

   Mounika has been a member of the community since 2014 and she writes flash fiction & experiences. Her works can be accessed at writerspouch.com/profile/12

4. **Nikhila Kotni**
   Contributor of "Negative Assumptions"

   Nikhila has been a member of the community since 2014 and she writes flash fiction, short stories & novelette. Her works can be accessed at writerspouch.com/profile/6

5. **Prakhyat Chatla**
   Contributor of "The Rat Race"

   Prakhyat has been a member of the community since 2015 and he writes poems & short stories. His works can be accessed at writerspouch.com/

profile/14

6. **Preety Singh**
   Contributor of "Mother's Day"

   Preety has been a member of the community since 2015 and she writes flash fiction. Her works can be accessed at writerspouch.com/profile/19

7. **R. S. Chintalapati**
   Contributor of "The Man Who Called Everyone Shiva" & "Winter's Whisper"

   Ravi is the founder of the community and he writes short stories & clicks pictures. His works can be accessed at writerspouch.com/profile/2

8. **Srilekha Kandarpa**
   Contributor of "Woman: A Fairy in Disguise"

   Srilekha has been a member of the community since 2013 and she writes experience. Her works can be accessed at writerspouch.com/profile/53

9. **Vaidurya Pratap Sahi**
   Contributor of "The Elephant Ride"

   Vaidurya has been a member of the community since 2019 and he writes chronicles & short stories. His works can be accessed at writerspouch.com/profile/35

About Editors

1. **R. K. Chamarla**
   Editor of "A Madrasi's Predicament", "Mother's Day" & "The Man Who Called Everyone Shiva"

   Raghuveer has been a member of the community since 2011 and he edits flash fictions and novelettes. His works can be accessed at writerspouch.com/profile/1

2. **Sreekar Ayyagari**
   Editor of "Amma's Special Box", "Daddy's Little Girl", "Histories", "My First Kiss", "Negative Assumptions", "The Elephant Ride", "The Rat Race" & "Winter's Whisper"

   Sreekar has been a member of the community since 2020 and he edits flash fictions and novelettes. His works can be accessed at writerspouch.com/profile/40

3. **Sree Raj**
   Editor of "Daddy's Little Girl" & "Winter's Whisper"

   Sree has been a member of the community since 2011 and he edits short stories and non-fiction. His works can be accessed at writerspouch.com/profile/4

About Photographers

1. **Pankaj Tottada**
   Photographer of "Daddy's Little Girl", "My First Kiss", "Negative Assumptions", & "The Rat Race"

   Pankaj has been a member of the community since 2015 and he has contributed numerous photographs. His contributions can be accessed at writerspouch.com/profile/13

2. **Prabhath Narapareddy**
   Photographer of "Woman: A Fairy in Disguise"

   Prabhath has been a member of the community since 2014 and he has contributed numerous photographs. His contributions can be accessed at writerspouch.com/profile/7

3. **Ravindra Patoju**
   Photographer of "Histories"

   Ravindra has been a member of the community since 2020 and he has contributed numerous photographs. His contributions can be accessed at writerspouch.com/profile/38

4. **R. S. Chintalapati**
   Photographer of "Amma's Special Box" &"Winter's Whisper"

   Ravi is the founder of the community and he writes short stories & clicks pictures. His works can be accessed at writerspouch.com/profile/2

About Illustrator

Vaidurya Pratap Sahi
Illustrator of "The Elephant Ride"

Vaidurya has been a member of the community since 2019 and he writes chronicles & short stories. His works can be accessed at writerspouch.com/profile/35

About Community

Writers Pouch is an Indian community that commissions various works of different art forms. Encompassing creators, contributors, editors, proofreaders, reviewers, photographers, and illustrators, the organisation aims to create unique forms of art in every genre.

Established in 2009, Writers Pouch started by publishing short stories, essays and poems. Later on, the organisation even started releasing novelettes, novellas, novels, book series, & non-fiction.

The goal of Writers Pouch is to explore art uniquely and this is accomplished by commissioning a group of artists on every project. They are a home for all creative individuals who are striving to tell their stories or ideas creatively while holding on to their principles.

If you loved our works, visit our website at writerspouch.com to buy our other titles.

1. I'm Your Loving Intern [2015]
2. Loving Intern [2016]
3. The Soul Snatchers [2016]
4. Broken Bonds [2017]
5. God's Council: The Four Auins [2017]
6. Your Loving Intern [2018]
7. Eternal Love [2019]
8. Burning Beacons [2020]
9. A Walk in Paradise [2020]
10. Immortal Verses [2020]
11. Eccentric Endings [2020]
12. Casket of Tales [2020]

Printed by Libri Plureos GmbH in Hamburg,
Germany

9 798885 553902